Doctor Doctor Jokes

Jokes by John Broadhead and Joyce McAleer
Cover by Paul Crompton
Cartoons by Walter Howarth

Copyright © 1991 World International Publishing Ltd.

All rights reserved. Published in Great Britain by
World International Publishing Ltd.,
an Egmont Company, Egmont House,
P.O. Box 111, Great Ducie Street,
Manchester M60 3BL.
Printed in Great Britain.

British Library Cataloguing in Publication Data
Broadhead, John
 Doctor, doctor joke book.
 1. Humorous prose
 I. Title II. McAleer, Joyce
 828.91402

ISBN 0 7498 0447 5

No part of this publication may be reproduced, stored
in a retrieval system, or transmitted, in any form or by
any means, electronic, mechanical, photocopying,
recording, or otherwise, without prior permission of
the copyright owners.

Doctor Doctor Jokes

World International Publishing
Limited Manchester

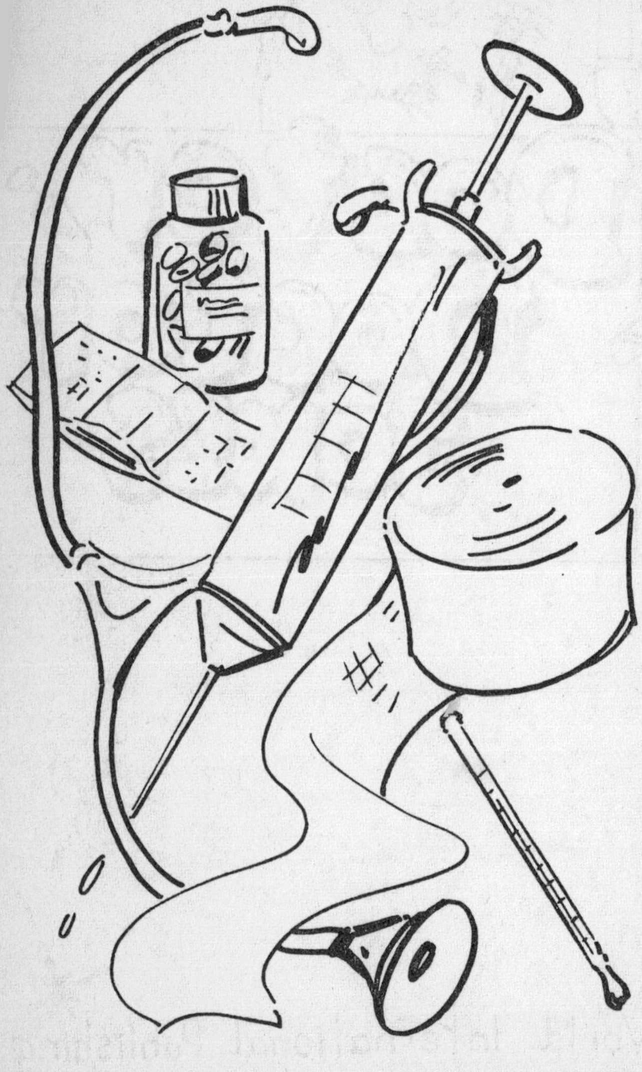

Doctor: 'What makes you think your husband is a chocoholic, Mrs Brown?'
Mrs Brown: 'He eats Easter eggs with his bacon and tomatoes, doctor!'

Who refused to treat James Bond?
   Dr No!

'Doctor! Doctor! I've swallowed a record-player needle . . . record-player needle . . . record-player needle . . .'

'Why are you so keen to work for the blood transfusion service, Nurse Blenkinsop?'

Mrs Smith: 'Help me, doctor! Little Tommy's swallowed the can-opener!'
Doctor: 'Don't panic — he'll be alright!'
Mrs Smith: 'But how do I open the beans? The toast's getting cold!'

Patient: (to cosmetic-surgeon) 'Will it hurt, doctor?'
Surgeon: 'Only when you get my bill, Mrs Brown!'

'Doctor! Doctor! What can I do about my terrible shyness?'
  'Come out from beneath the bed and I'll tell you!'

Worried secretary: (speaking on the phone) 'My boss has been flattened by a steam-roller, doctor! Can you help him?'
Doctor: 'Certainly! Fax him to my surgery immediately!'

'Doctor! Doctor! I think I'm a roll of film.'
  'Well take these pills with water and we'll see how things develop.'

'Is it serious, doctor?'
'Well, I wouldn't bother booking any holidays this year!'

Mum: 'I'm worried about my son Jimmy. He keeps talking to the Alsatian dog across the road!'
Doctor: 'Sounds harmless enough to me . . .'
Mum: 'But I can't afford the phone bills!'

Doctor: 'You're remarkably lucky for a man who's fallen off a ladder . . .'
Joe: 'I was only standing on the first rung, doctor!'

Mrs Dodds: 'Doctor! Doctor! I keep talking to myself!'
Doctor: 'Don't worry, Mrs Dodds. Lots of people do that!'
Mrs Dodds: 'There you are, you silly woman! I told you the doctor would understand!'

'Doctor! Doctor! One of my legs is shorter than the other! What can I do?'
'Try walking with one foot in the gutter!'

Which doctor has all the time in the world for you?
  Doctor Who!

Timmy: 'Doctor, is it usual for parents to pass things down to their children?'
Doctor: 'Yes, there are many hereditary factors . . .'
Timmy: 'Good! I'm hoping my dad will leave me his gold watch!'

'Is it serious, doctor?'
  'Let me put it this way — have you ever heard of the Black Death?'

What is the medical term for a person who has swallowed a bottle of poison?
  Dead!

Kevin: 'Ho, ho! Hee, hee! I just can't stop laughing, doctor!'
Doctor: 'Goodness me, how long have you been like this?'
Kevin: 'Only since I came into the surgery.'
Doctor: 'Hmmm . . . I wonder why?'
Kevin: 'Because your wig's falling off!'

Doctor: 'Did you know that there are more than 1,000 bones in the human body?'
Tom: 'Shhh, doctor! My dog's outside in the waiting room!'

'Congratulations, Mr Brown — you're in great shape for a man of sixty. Pity you're only forty!'

Definition of a stethoscope:
  A long rubber tube with a doctor at the other end!

What do you call a man who swallows his tax-demand?
  Bill!

'Operator, operator — call me an ambulance!'
'Okay, Sir — you're an ambulance!'

Why are patients so-called?
Because they have to wait patiently for treatment!

'Doctor! Doctor! I feel threatened all the time . . .'
'Shut up or you'll be sorry!'

Harry: 'Can you help me, doctor? I'm only five feet tall . . .'
Doctor: 'Nurse — fetch a stretcher for this patient!'

'Doctor! Doctor! I feel as if I'm living in the past . . .'
'Don't worry, Mr Dobson, many people do that as they grow older. By the way, have you heard how Nelson's getting on at Trafalgar?'

'Doctor! Doctor! I feel like a goose — and I'm sick of it!'
'Now, now, don't duck the issue!'

Doctor: 'I'm thinking of putting you on a staple diet.'
Susie: 'Not likely — they'll stick in my throat!'

Doctor: 'It looks as if you have shingles, Mr Shaw.'
Mr Shaw: 'But I've not been anywhere near the sea, doctor!'

'Don't you think you should cut down on watching television, Mr Brown?'

P.C. Bloggs: 'I can't get rid of these dark rings round my eyes. What should I do?'
Doctor: 'Apply for a panda car!'

Mavis: 'My daughter believes in preventative medicine, doctor.'
Doctor: 'Oh, really?'
Mavis: 'Yes — she tries to prevent me from making her take it!'

'Doctor! Doctor! I couldn't swallow those big white pills you gave me.'
  'Ah, so that's what happened to my golf-balls!'

Doctor: 'Will you take part in some experimental medicine, my dear?'
Madge: 'Of course, doctor.'
Doctor: 'Good. Hang this dead mouse round your neck and sleep with this toad under your pillow for a week!'

What's the difference between a good doctor and a bad one?
  One treats ills, and the other ill-treats!

Charles: 'Nice painting you have there, doctor.'
Doctor: 'Yes, a patient left it to me.'
Charles: 'Nice pen you're writing with.'
Doctor: 'Yes, another patient left it to me.'
Charles: 'I've got a terrible pain in my chest, doctor.'
Doctor: 'Nice gold watch you're wearing!'

Patient: 'Every time I try to stroke a cat I get an upset stomach, doctor.'
Doctor: 'Don't worry. It's just a gut reaction.'

Nurse: 'Is Doctor Smith permanently drunk? He always sways down the ward, grabbing hold of the end of each bed.'
Sister: 'No, he used to be a ship's doctor!'

Doctor: 'Oh, it's you yet again, Mr Ferret!'
Mr Ferret: 'Yes, I have a pain in the neck, doctor.'
Doctor: 'You are a pain in the neck!'

Edna: 'Is artificial colouring harmful?'
Doctor: 'So some people say — but only in large quantities.'
Edna: 'Phew, that's a relief! I've discovered I used a tin of black gloss paint instead of treacle when I baked my tarts yesterday!'

Doctor: 'Ah, did you cure your nose-bleed by dropping a cold key down your back, as I suggested?'
Johnny: 'Yes, but now I've caught a cold because I've been locked out all day!'

Doctor: 'I'm afraid your gums are receding, Carol.'
Carol: 'Phew, what a relief! I thought my teeth were growing longer!'

Musician: 'All this trumpet playing is making me crotchety, doctor . . .'
Doctor: 'Well, brève more deeply, take a long rest for a minim of two weeks, and don't go in to bars!'

Doctor: 'Hmmm . . . you seem to have rather a lot of dandruff, Mrs Porter . . .'
Mrs P: 'That's not dandruff, doctor — the baby threw porridge at me this morning!'

'Help me, doctor! I think someone's following me!'
'Well, they'll just have to wait their turn! I can only see one patient at a time!'

'Doctor! Doctor! I've got jug ears!'
'Well, sit down and pour out your story to me!'

What do you call a man who's swallowed a rabbit?
  Warren!

'Help, doctor! I can't breathe!'
'No wonder, Mr Green — your tie's caught on the door handle!'

'Doctor! Doctor! I've got horrible cold shivers running down my back!'
'Oh, dear! The waiting room ceiling must be leaking again!'

The doctor came out to speak to an expectant father pacing up and down anxiously in the waiting room.

'Mr Jones, the nurse has something for you . . .' he said.

'Oh, dear!' sighed Mr Jones frantically. 'What shall we call it?!'

'How about "a cup of tea"?' replied the puzzled doctor as the nurse walked in with a hot drink for Mr Jones.

'Doctor! Doctor! If I eat only lettuce and raw carrots, will I live to be 100?'

'No, but it will certainly seem like it!'

'Help! The doctor says I only have 59 seconds to live!'

'Just wait a minute!'

The place where they're building the new optician's department is a site for sore eyes!

'Doctor! Doctor! I think I have tunnel vision!'

'Really? You should become an engine driver!'

'Do you smoke, Mr Jones?'

'No idea, doctor. Nobody's ever set fire to me!'

A young lady runs into hospital and rushes up to the nearest man in a white coat.

'Help me!' she cries. 'I've broken out all over in spots!'

'Oh, dear!'

'And look, my tongue's all furry!'

'How awful!'

'I'm aching all over . . . my vision's blurred . . . and I'm out of breath. Am I going to die?'

'How should I know, Miss? I'm only the painter and decorator!'

Why is medicine like ice-cream?

They both make you shiver when you swallow them!

'Doctor! Doctor! My wife's growing a large bushy beard!'

'You're lucky! My wife's useless in the garden — she can't even grow daisies!'

Alf: 'Those sleeping tablets you told me to take are playing havoc with my work.'
Doctor: 'How strange! What's your job?'
Alf: 'I'm a night watchman!'

'Doctor! Doctor! I'm only four feet tall and addicted to sugar. Is there a name for my condition!'

'Yes — short and sweet!'

'My, Mr Jones, what big eyes you've got . . . my, Mr Jones, what big teeth you've got . . . my, Mr Jones, what shaggy hair you've got . . . I think it's the vet you want to see, Mr Jones!'

'Now, what seems to be the problem?'

Doctor: 'I'm going to have to watch your wife's figure very carefully, Mr Smith . . .'
Smith: 'Rather you than me, doctor!'

Pilot: 'Doctor, I've drunk some aviation fuel by mistake! What'll I do?'
Doctor: 'Oh, about 500 mph, I should say!'

Johnny: 'How can I lose twelve pounds of ugly fat?'
Doctor: 'Cut your head off!'

Surgeon: 'No need to worry about your operation, madam — I've been practising for twenty years . . .'
Patient: 'What?! In that case I'll come back when you're ready!'

Terry: 'It's the glasses, doctor . . . they're making this red mark on my nose.'
Doctor: 'But you have perfect eyesight!'
Terry: 'I mean beer glasses, doctor!'

What's the cure for water on the brain?
A tap on the head!

Doctor: 'You're suffering from athlete's foot, tennis elbow and housemaid's knee . . .'
Patient: 'Then sign me off the sick quickly, doctor! With all those qualifications I should soon find a job!'

'Witch doctor! Witch doctor! My neighbours are making me ill . . .'
   'Then stop eating them!'

'I don't know why they say these tablets are addictive. I've been taking them for over thirty years and I'm not addicted yet!'

Nurse: 'One of the patients says he's hungry, doctor.'
Doctor: 'Which one?'
Nurse: 'Mr Robinson, with the pigeon-toes.'
Doctor: 'Throw him some bread!'

Ron: 'My wife gets pins and needles every time I go shopping.'
Doctor: 'You're lucky! My wife usually gets a new outfit!'

Clown: 'I'm better now, doctor – I think I'll go back to work . . .'
Doctor: 'Now that would be a daft thing to do!'

Doctor: (alone with patient) 'I think you're suffering from double vision, Mr Smith.'
Mr Smith: 'Nonsense! I demand a second opinion from your colleague sitting next to you!'

Patient: 'Doctor, will I have to have jabs before I go on my tropical holiday?'
Doctor: 'Yes — come back for them tomorrow.'
Patient: 'No, thanks — I'll go to Blackpool instead!'

What's the best thing for kleptomania?
  A fast getaway car!

Prisoner: 'Look here, doc! You've already removed my spleen, tonsils, adenoids and one of my kidneys. I only came to see if you could get me out of this place!'
Prison Doctor: 'I am – bit by bit!'

'Doctor! Doctor! I keep thinking I'm a door knob!'
  'What's the matter? Can't you handle it!'

Gladys: 'I'm annoyed, doctor — you told my husband he'd be healthier if he bought a big dog and took it for walks . . .'
Doctor: 'Well?'
Gladys: 'It ate him yesterday!'

Patient: (being examined) 'Doctor, why does everybody laugh at me?'
Doctor: 'I . . . I . . . ha, ha! Oh, do excuse me . . . ho, ho! I don't really . . . tee, hee . . . know!'

'Doctor, my wife's cooking is making me ill. What's the cure?'
   'Divorce, of course!'

Doctor: 'Next patient, please . . . hello, there!'
Gladys: 'Don't mind if I do.'
Doctor: 'Now, you must be Gladys Brown . . . ?'
Gladys: 'No, I came on the bus.'
Doctor: 'Do sit down . . .'
Gladys: 'Yes, please — two sugars.'
Doctor: (yelling) 'You've come about your DEAFNESS, right?'
Gladys: 'Oooh, what a clever doctor! However did you know that just by looking at me?!'

I. HACKETT
TREE SURGEON
BRANCHES THROUGHOUT
THE U.K.

'Doctor, my husband treats me like a dog . . .'
   'Try biting his ankles!'

Doctor: 'Not seen you for a while, Mr Jones.'
Mr Jones: 'No, doctor, I've been ill!'

Gertie: 'I'm still going skiing despite what you say, doctor.'
Doctor: 'Well, don't come running to me when you break your legs!'

Boy: 'Doctor! Doctor! I think I'm an ancient Egyptian king.'
Doctor: 'What has your mummy got to say about this?'

'Doctor! Doctor! My knees are turning blue.'
'Your kilt's too short, Mr MacTavish!'

'Doctor! Doctor! I keep dreaming I'm in hot water with pieces of meat and vegetables in it.'
'Oh, dear. You are in a stew!'

Maisie: 'So what's wrong, doctor?'
Doctor: 'Have you heard of St Vitus' Dance?'
Maisie: 'What kind of doctor are you? I came here for treatment — not to discuss my social life!'

Ivy: 'Doctor, I've got a bad chest!'
Doctor: 'What's wrong with it?'
Ivy: 'The lock's broken!'

'Doctor! Doctor! I keep thinking I'm a frog.'
   'Just hop up on to the couch.'

'Doctor! Doctor! The neighbours are making me sick!'
   'Switch to another channel then!'

'Come on, man! Have you no guts?'

'Doctor, I just hate my boss. What should I do?'
'Spit him out at once!'

What did the hypnotist say to Dr Jekyll?
You are getting . . . very . . . creepy!

Teenager: 'I'm losing the feeling in my legs.'
Doctor: 'No wonder — your jeans are too tight!'

'Doctor! Doctor! I keep falling out with my wife!'
'Well, stop sleeping in that silly hammock!'

'I must be allergic to work, doctor. Whenever I think about it, I come out in a rash!'

Doctor: 'Your sore needs treating twice a day, Julie.'
Julie: 'Right, I'll buy it a box of chocs this afternoon . . . and I'll take it to the pictures this evening!'

Absent-minded surgeon sitting next to a nurse in hospital dining-room after a hard day:
'Knife . . . fork . . . vinegar . . . scalpel . . .'

Knock! Knock!
Who's there?
Doctor!
Doctor Who?
Yes — were you expecting me?!

What do you call a GP who only comes out at night?
   Docula!

McDuff, the world champion caber-tosser, ran out of the doctor's surgery in tears.
   'What did you say to him, doc?' asked his friend.
   'Oh, I just told him never to lift anything heavy!'

'Doctor! Doctor! I'm going bald!'
   'Oh, well — hair today, gone tomorrow!'

New receptionist to old receptionist: 'Doctor Sawyer's blaming me for people disappearing! I overheard him saying he's losing his patients more and more since I came to work here!'

Heard about the two-faced doctor? He signed the Hypocritic Oath!

'Doctor! Doctor! I keep imagining I'm famous . . .'

'Before I examine you, Mr Jones, may I have your autograph?'

What do you call a girl who's swallowed her pocket money?

Penny!

Patient: 'Oh, I feel dreadful . . . my head hurts, my eyes ache . . .'
Doctor: 'And your neck feels swollen . . . ?'
Patient: 'Yes!'
Doctor: 'Finding it difficult to swallow, too?'
Patient: 'Yes!'
Doctor: 'Indigestion after every meal?'
Patient: 'Exactly, doctor! What is it?'
Doctor: 'Haven't a clue. I've had it all week myself!'

Hypnotist to patient in a trance: 'My fees are very reasonable . . . my fees are very reasonable . . . !'

Where do chocolate cream cakes go when they're poorly?

Black Forest Clinic!

'Doctor! Doctor! Why have people got belly-buttons?'

'Well, Johnny, when God finishes making people, he stands them in a line and pokes them in the tummy, saying, "You're done . . . you're done . . . and you're done!"'

What do you call a girl who eats flowers?
   Daisy!

The busy nurse pops the thermometer in Mr Smith's mouth and then disappears. She doesn't return for half an hour.

'Are you the nurse who put the thermometer in my mouth?' asks Mr Smith.

'Yes, I am,' replies the puzzled nurse.

'Really?! I was expecting someone much older!'

'What do you call a girl who can't sleep and gets up early every morning?'
Dawn!

Bob: 'When my brother went into hospital, they removed his nose by mistake.'
Ted: 'How does he smell?'
Bob: 'Terrible!'

Little Billy was rushed into the hospital casualty department on a stretcher.
'Help him, doctor! He's swallowed the telephone!'
The doctor sounded his chest carefully and shook his head gravely. 'I'm afraid you shouldn't have dialled 999, madam. You want the engineer on 151 — I can't get a dialling tone!'

Patient: 'Well, doctor, how long have I got to live?'
Doctor: 'About half an hour!'
Patient: 'That's terrible! Is there nothing you can do for me?'
Doctor: 'Well, there is one thing . . . go and ask my receptionist to show you her holiday photos of Majorca. It'll make half an hour seem like a lifetime!'

Tommy: 'Doctor! Doctor! Will I be able to play the piano when you take the plaster cast off my broken wrist?'
Doctor: 'Of course you will, Tommy.'
Tommy: 'That's funny. I've never been able to play it up to now!'

Twitty doctor: 'You have a chill on your kiddlies, Mrs Robinson.'
Mrs Robinson: 'Don't you mean my kidneys, doctor?'
Doctor: 'I said kiddlies, diddle I?'

Smoothie psychiatrist to nervous patient: 'Now, now, Mr Robinson, it's not flying you're afraid of — it's crashing!'

'Mrs Jones, what gives you the idea that your sleeping-pills are too strong? Mrs Jones . . . Mrs Jones . . . wake up, Mrs Jones!'

Doctor: 'Hmm, you have a superficial laceration to the epidermis of your olfactory organ . . .'
Hypochondriac: 'Oh, no! What does that mean in simple terms?'
Doctor: 'A small scratch on your nose!'

'Doctor! Doctor! My husband says he can't stand the sight of me! Can you prescribe anything for him!'
  'Yes — my sympathy!'

'My wife's on a new low-fat diet. She sits on the floor and eats bags of chips!'

Bob: 'Doctor! Doctor! I think I'm ugly . . .'
Doctor: 'Okay, go and stand behind the screen, please.'
Bob: 'D'you need to examine me?'
Doctor: 'No, I just can't stand the sight of you!'

'Doctor! Doctor! Will my treatment be expensive?'
  'Be with you in a moment, Mrs Jones . . . I've just left my Rolls on the double yellow lines!'

George: 'I'm fed up, doc — I've been walking the streets all day . . .'
Doctor: 'Oh, dear! Let's try to find the cause of your depression. First of all, what's your job?'
George: 'I'm a postman!'

Patient: 'If you don't mind me saying so, doctor, you haven't a very sympathetic manner . . .'
Doctor: 'What d'you mean by that, you potty old hypochondriac? Now, clear off!'

'Doctor! Doctor! My baby won't stop crying! What do you recommend?'
　'Earplugs!'

New hospital patient: 'I believe you're a bit overcrowded at the moment . . .'
Admissions clerk: 'Don't worry about it! Just pitch this tent round the back!'

What's the best cure for indigestion?
　Starvation!

Hypnotist: 'Okay, Mr Henry, when I say "wake up" you will no longer be shy but full of confidence and be able to speak your mind . . . wake up!'
Patient: 'Right, you! How about giving me a refund, you money-grabbing old skinflint!'

'Doctor! Doctor! I've developed a passion for duck eggs! What's your opinion?'
'You must have gone quackers!'

'Doctor! Doctor! I've become obsessed with television . . . I watch it 24 hours a day!'
'Oh, good! How did last night's film end?!'

What's the best way to overcome car-sickness?
Go by train!

Mrs Robinson: 'Doctor, that medicine you prescribed has brought me out in spots! I've a good mind to sue you . . .'
Doctor: 'Now, Mrs Robinson, don't be so rash!'

Doctor: 'Morning, Mr Smith! Did you know it's St Patrick's Day today?'
Mr Smith: 'Oh, you'd best deal with him today then. I'll come back tomorrow!'

Patient: 'Doctor! Doctor! Whenever I have a bath, I catch cold.'
Doctor: 'Is your bathroom heated?'
Patient: 'Yes, but the hot tap doesn't work!'

'Been eating your home-grown mushrooms again, Mr Walker?'

Mrs Jones: 'Is the doctor a good one?'
Receptionist: 'Yes — he's an unqualified success!'
Mrs Jones: 'Oh, that's no use . . . I want a proper doctor!'

Doctor: 'That's a bad lump on your head, Mr Jay.'
Mr Jay: 'Yes, doctor. My wife did it.'
Doctor: 'Whatever for?'
Mr Jay: 'I said that if she could cook breakfast without burning it, pigs would fly.'
Doctor: 'And?'
Mr Jay: 'She said pigs *would* fly — then threw a pound of pork sausages at me!'

'Ah, you must be Mr Bendini, the trapeze artist!'

Miss Proudfoot: 'I'm obsessed with the handsome man who lives opposite. And now he's accusing me of spying on him!'
Doctor: 'Can't you avoid looking at him?'
Miss Proudfoot: 'Only if I don't stand on the dressing table with my binoculars!'

Cannibal: 'I've got awful indigestion . . .'
Witch doctor: 'Oh, dear! You must have eaten someone that disagreed with you!'

'Doctor! Doctor! I've eaten ten bowls of jelly. Will I be alright?'
  'Just wobble over here while I examine you!'

Tom: 'What's good for excessive wind, doctor?'
Doctor: 'A kite!'

Tom: 'My tongue's full of splinters, doctor . . .'
Doctor: 'You've been eating too many chips!'

What d'you call a man who's swallowed a tree?
  Lumbered!

'Do you find it difficult passing water, Mr Sozzle?'
'No, doctor. But I do find it hard to pass a pub!'

'Doctor! Doctor! I feel as if I'm changing into a grandfather clock . . .'
  'Well, I've noticed you have a nervous tic!'

What d'you call a girl who's swallowed the complete works of Shakespeare?
   Greedy!

What do you call a boy who's swallowed his pocket money?
   Broke!

Bedridden patient: 'Help, nurse! Call the doctor!'
Nurse: 'Okay — I hate him, the good-for-nothing, pompous, conceited old windbag!'

'Good news and bad news, Mr Ashworth! The good news is that you'll have a full head of hair again in six months. The bad news is — you've only got three months to live!'

What do you give the man who's got everything?
   A chemist's shop!

How would you describe a woman who's swallowed a bar of soap?
   Bubbly!

'Oo-er, is it yellow fever, doctor?'
'No, you're just a complete coward!'

Madge: 'Doctor, is it true that eating carrots helps you to see in the dark?'
Doctor: 'There is some truth in that . . .'
Madge: 'Good. I'm trying to save on electricity!'

'Doctor! Doctor! I feel like an ant!'
'Life can be all uphill at times!'

'Would you mind asking the doctor to look at my case again?!'

Mr Wimp: 'Doctor, if I changed my name, would it make me more forceful and dynamic?'
Doctor: 'What name did you have in mind?'
Mr Wimp: 'Napoleon Bonaparte!'

Nurse: 'Doctor! Doctor! I've given Mr Brown hydrogen instead of oxygen!'
Doctor: 'Well?'
Nurse: 'He's just floated away through the window!'

What disease should you have before you join the European Community?
  German measles!

'Doctor! Doctor! I feel like a teapot . . .'
  'Oh, do stop spouting about yourself!'

Dick: 'Remember you told me to beat depression by going out and enjoying myself?'
Doctor: 'Of course. Did you take my advice?'
Dick: 'Yes, but I feel much worse now. When I got home, my wife hit me with the rolling pin!'

'Doctor! Doctor! How can you tell if you're a genius?'
  'Easy! I've always known I was!'

'Doctor! Doctor! I feel like a pair of glasses.'
  'Sit down and stop making a spectacle of yourself.'

Why do surgeons wear a mask and rubber gloves during operations?
  To avoid leaving incriminating evidence if anything goes wrong!

'Help me, doctor — I can't give up smoking!'

'Doctor! Doctor! I keep dreaming I'm in my pram!'
'Oh, *do* grow up, Mr Jones!'

'Doctor! Doctor! What can I do about my bald head?'
'Wipe it once a day with a damp cloth!'

Flo: 'Are showers good for you, doctor?'
Doctor: 'Yes, they're very refreshing.'
Flo: 'Good. It's raining and I've forgotten my umbrella!'

Doctor: 'It is my opinion, my dear fellow, that you are malingering badly . . .'
Bill: 'Am I really, doctor? Looks as if I'd better stay off for another week then!'

Patient: 'Nurse, I'm having a terrible job swallowing this aspirin . . .'
Nurse: 'I'm not surprised. That's the cotton wool from the top of the bottle!'

Harry: 'Can you help me overcome my terribly jealous nature?'
Doctor: 'Yes, I'll send you to a specialist. Is that okay?'
Harry: 'A specialist? Certainly not — I'd make a better doctor than you lot any day!'

'Doctor! Doctor! Is there anything I can buy to make me look taller?'
   'Yes, a pair of step-ladders!'

What's the difference between catarrh and a guitar?
   One makes you feel like sniffing, and the other makes you feel like skiffling!

Sister: 'Help, doctor — I've some patients missing. There are only twenty in the ward, not twenty-six, as you told me . . .'
Doctor: 'Calm down, sister — I said twenty *sick* patients!'

'Doctor! Doctor! This infernal rain is getting on my nerves!'
   'Calm down. You're simply under the weather!'

Bill: 'Why do I have spots before the eyes?'
Doctor: 'Try cleaning your specs!'

'Doctor! Doctor! I'm losing my memory. What can I do?'
 'Oh, try to forget about it!'

Doctor: 'Before I give you the results of your tests, Mr Thompson, just fill in this . . .'
Thompson: 'What is it?'
Doctor: 'Your will!'

'Doctor! Doctor! I've won a fortune on the pools but I can't stand the responsibility! Can you help me out?'
 'Certainly — here's my bill for £50,000!'

Geoff: 'I've started getting dizzy at work, doctor . . .'
Doctor: 'Well, just sit down whenever it happens.'
Geoff: 'I can't — I'm a tightrope walker!'

Doctor: 'This patient has a very strange blood group . . .'
Nurse: 'Silly! That's the cherryade from his bedside table!'

Anxious woman
on phone: 'Doctor, I sent my husband to the shops for a cauliflower but he's tripped on the pavement and twisted his ankle. What should I do?'
Doctor: 'Open a tin of peas!'

Chatterbox: 'Morning, doctor. Lovely day. How's the wife? How are the kids? How's business? Are you well? I've already got my holidays booked for the summer . . .'
Doctor: 'Stop talking, please, Mr Smith, and open wide . . . ah, you have an extremely furry tongue! I wonder why that is . . . ?'
Chatterbox: ''Cos you keep telling me to put a sock in it!'

Patient: 'I'd like to get married but I haven't found the right man . . .'
Receptionist: 'Oh, our Dr Frankenstein will make a lovely husband for you!'

'My doctor's getting very absent-minded. When I asked him the time, he said it was just gone septic!'

'Doctor! Doctor! I feel like an electric socket . . .'
   'Oh, put a plug in it!'

Bill: 'My wife beats me, doctor!'
Doctor: 'Oh, dear! How often?'
Bill: 'Every time we play Scrabble!'

Kate: 'In my opinion, doctor, you don't know what you're talking about.'
Doctor: 'How long have you been having these strange delusions?'

Mrs Worthington: 'Do you have time for a talk, doctor?'
Doctor: 'All the time in the world, madam.'
Mrs Worthington: 'Good, come to the Women's Institute coffee morning in ten minutes. The ladies are waiting for a lecture!'

Mary: 'Is swimming good for you, doctor?'
Doctor: 'Yes, it's an excellent form of exercise . . .'
Mary: 'Good. My goldfish should live for years and years then!'

Doctor: 'How long has your husband been a hypochondriac, Annie?'
Annie: 'Since his last birthday . . . the day I gave him his present — a first aid manual!'

Two hard-up old men, Albert and Herbert, dodder past a doctor's surgery which reads 'Dr Brown will knock 50 years off your age for just £10'.

'I'll try it first,' says Albert, 'and if it's any good, I'll lend you the money to go in.'

Five minutes later Albert trots out of the surgery, looking about eighteen — tall, straight and with sleek black hair.

'You look great!' cries Albert. 'Lend me some money!'

'Clear off, you old pauper!' says Herbert, pushing him aside and marching off.

'Doctor! Doctor! I must have eaten too many eggs! I overheard a neighbour saying that I was hard-boiled!'

Doctor: 'How are the kids?'
Farmer Giles: 'Oh, they're fine, doctor. They're all growing nice long beards — and so is Nanny!'
Doctor: 'What?! You'd better bring them in to see me immediately!'
Farmer Giles: 'Don't be silly, doctor! How am I going to get four goats in here?!'

Nurse: (wheeling patient into the theatre) 'Why so worried? It's only a minor operation.'
Quivering patient: 'I think it's something to do with that vulture perched over the door!'

'Don't worry, Harry, it's not yellow fever . . .
my fluorescent light's on the blink!'

Doctor: 'Do you like fishing?'
Joe: 'Yes, I love it.'
Doctor: 'Good — you've got worms!'

What d'you call a man who's swallowed an elephant?
   Amazing!

Doctor: 'This is most peculiar . . . you appear to have distemper! Are you a dog-lover, by any chance?'
Patient: 'Not likely! If a dog comes near me, I bite *it* first!'

Farmer Giles: 'I've got an awful buzzin' in me ears, doc!'
Doctor: 'And a wasp's nest in your hair, too!'

Patient: 'Doctor! Doctor! I have a strange aversion to the telephone!'
Doctor: 'Why is that?'
Patient: 'I can't pay the bill!'

Miss Trimble: 'I get drunk so easily, doctor . . .'
Doctor: 'Try cutting down then.'
Miss Trimble: 'Right — I'll only buy two packets of wine gums a day, instead of three!'

'Doctor! Doctor! I feel like a kangaroo . . .'
  'Oh, hop it!'

Tomkins: 'I'm so worried, doctor. My wife's left me . . .'
Doctor: 'Oh, she'll come back.'
Tomkins: 'That's what worries me!'

'Doctor! Doctor! Is it serious?'
  'Well, put it this way. I wouldn't bother starting to read *The Rise and Fall of The Roman Empire!*'

Dick: 'Doctor, I think the kipper I had for breakfast this morning was a bit off. It was very bright in colour.'
Doctor: 'Don't worry. It was probably just a red herring!'

What d'you call a man with a scalp disease?
  Dan Druff!

Mary: 'Doctor, I think I'm addicted to caffeine.'
Doctor: 'Let's examine your symptoms. For instance, do you long for a cup of tea?'
Mary: 'Yes please, doctor — with milk and two sugars!'

'Doctor! Doctor! How can I look more feminine?'
  'I'm afraid you'd need a sex change, Mr Smith!'

Ivy: 'Doctor, do you think there's an afterlife . . . where you'll meet all your past patients again?'
Doctor: 'If there is, I'll have to avoid a few of them!'

Patient: 'Nurse, you've bandaged the wrong leg!'
Nurse: 'No, I've bandaged the right leg . . .'
Patient: 'Yes, but it should have been the left one!'

'Doctor! Doctor! I'm going mouldy!'
  'That's okay — you can join the Green Party!'

'Doctor! Doctor! I feel like I'm a Christmas turkey!'
'Oh, stuff and nonsense!'

'Doctor! Doctor! Whenever I hear a knock at the door, I get all nervous and have to hide under the bed . . . !'
'Don't worry, that's a very common complaint here in the prison hospital!'

What d'you call a man who's swallowed a flea?
Tickled pink!

What d'you call a girl who keeps swallowing school textbooks?
A glutton for learning!

'No, Mr Smith, I said take up *exercising* — not exorcising!'

Tommy: 'My dad saw red when I spat out my cherry-flavoured medicine.'
Doctor: 'Well, I suppose he was annoyed.'
Tommy: 'No, it splashed all over his specs!'

Tony: 'I'm terrified of flying!'
Doctor: 'That's very common.'
Tony: 'But I'm an airline pilot!'

'Doctor! Doctor! I've taken your advice about eating plenty of green vegetables, but I think I've gone too far! When I stand at a road junction, the traffic starts to move!'

Fifi: 'Doctor, you're the best-looking man I ever saw!'
Doctor: 'How nice of you, my dear! Now, what's your problem?'
Fifi: 'Blurred vision!'

'Doctor! Doctor! The weather's getting me down. What can I do?'
  'Emigrate!'

'Doctor! Doctor! My wife doesn't understand me!'
  'No wonder — she's Chinese!'

Bill: 'I have this recurring nightmare where a huge monkey eats me . . .'
Doctor: 'You must be nuts!'

Worried patient: (on phone) 'Doctor, how can I tell if the berries I've just eaten are poisonous?'
Doctor: 'Well, if you wake up in the morning, come and see me!'

'Doctor! Doctor! I'd like to look like one of the famous stars.'
   'You already do — the Great Bear!'

'My sister's got such a crush on our new doctor that she's stopped eating apples in case it keeps him away!'

What d'you call a girl who's swallowed her dinner?
   Full up!

What d'you call a girl who's swallowed her friend's dinner as well?
   Greedy!

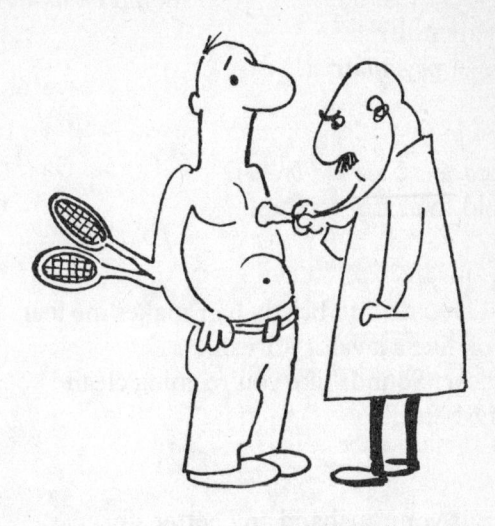

'Looks like you have tennis elbow, Mr Swift!'

Receptionist: 'Doctor, the invisible man's here for a check-up . . .'
Busy doctor: 'Tell him I can't see him!'

'Doctor! Doctor! Can you recommend a diet that isn't too strict?'
　'Sure! Eat as much as you like but don't swallow!'

Madge: 'Doctor, my son wants to become a busy G.P. just like you. Who should he talk to about it?'
Doctor: 'A psychiatrist!'

Why do doctors wear red braces?
  To hold their trousers up!

'Doctor! Doctor! My bristly hair makes me feel as if I look like a lavatory brush . . .'
  'Oh, dear! Sounds like you're going clean round the bend!'

Doctor: 'Is your husband any better since he started working for the AA?'
Kath: 'Not really. I'm afraid he's heading for yet another breakdown!'

'Doctor! Doctor! Everyone treats me like a dog.'
  'Sit . . . sit! There's a good boy!'

Henry: 'If I keep imagining everything will be alright, will it be?'
Psychiatrist: 'Yes — think positive!'
Henry: 'Great! I'll start imagining I didn't just bump your car outside!'

Doctor: 'How's the wife?'
Reg: 'Not very well. She was run over by a car . . .'
Doctor: 'How terrible! Was it serious?'
Reg: 'Not too bad — a bent bumper and a smashed headlamp!'

What d'you call a boy who's swallowed his homework?
  In trouble!

Mr Robinson: 'There's something wrong with me, doctor. I can't help setting fire to buildings . . .'
Psychiatrist: 'Ah, I like to see a man with burning ambition!'

'Doctor! Doctor! I feel like a camel. But I don't suppose you'll be able to help me . . .'
  'Now, now, don't get the hump!'

Nurse: 'This patient has the strongest pulse I've ever taken, doctor . . .'
Doctor: 'No wonder — you're feeling his wristwatch!'

'Doctor! Doctor! I have a phobia about going to school! Is it serious?'
  'In your case, yes. *You're* the headmaster!'

Flo: 'I think my new hearing aid is faulty . . .'
Doctor: 'Why do you say that?'
Flo: 'I keep on getting the all-clear to land from air traffic control!'

'No, Mr Felicini, I said "*say* 99"!'

'Doctor! Doctor! I'm always hungry.'
  'Oh, use your loaf, man!'

Doctor: 'I urge you to lose some weight before your next appointment, Mr Johnson.'
Mr Johnson: 'For the sake of my health?'
Doctor: 'No, because you've just broken my scales!'

1st Witch: 'I'm so fed up with my doctor, I'd like to change him?'
2nd Witch: 'Really?'
1st Witch: 'Yes — into a frog!'

'Doctor! Doctor! Have you any idea why so many ignorant, brainless, petty-minded, foolish people think I'm arrogant?!'

Quentin: 'Doctor! Doctor! Baby's just eaten the paper!'
Doctor: 'Not to worry . . . he'll be alright.'
Quentin: 'But I hadn't finished the crossword!'

Vera: 'Let me get this straight, doctor — a pacemaker makes the heart work regularly?'
Doctor: 'Quite right.'
Vera: 'Well, please fit one to my husband — he's been in and out of jobs ever since I married him!'

What d'you call a man who's swallowed a brush?
  Foxy!

'Doctor! Doctor! My neighbour's puppy has chewed my wooden leg and my spare one, too. Should I take him to court?'
  'I honestly doubt that you'll have a leg to stand on!'

'This is a very serious case, nurse!'

Mrs Sharples: 'My son is so inconsiderate, doctor. He only visits me once a year . . .'
Doctor: 'Oh, dear! I'll give him a ring. Where does he live?'
Mrs Sharples: 'Australia!'

Billy: 'I don't know why my teeth are so bad, doctor. I eat an apple a day!'
Doctor: 'Yes, but it's not supposed to be a toffee apple!'

'Doctor! Doctor! I think I'm suffering from housemaid's knee! Is it a common complaint?'
'Not among chartered accountants!'

'Doctor! Doctor! I get a funny gurgling sound in my stomach whenever I eat fish. What is it?'
'Sole music!'

What's the difference between the doctor and the gas board?
One mends ills, the other sends bills!

Why are surgeons like police informers?
They both stitch you up!

'Doctor! Doctor! I feel such a lemon all the time!'
  'Well, don't get sour about it!'

'Doctor Scrooge — I can't stop eating black-and-white striped mints. What d'you think!'
  'Humbug!'

Doctor: 'I think you should walk to work every morning.'
Sally: 'Will it make me slim and fit?'
Doctor: 'Yes.'
Sally: 'Funny — I only live over the shop!'

'Doctor! Doctor! I like to pretend I'm still a schoolboy. What should I do?'
  'Sit down, pay attention — and stop flicking paper pellets at me!'

What d'you call a man who hurts himself trying to lift his car?
  Jack!

Joyce: 'Are there any side effects with this medicine?'
Doctor: 'None at all — just terrible after effects!'

Albert: 'Can you give me anything for my liver?'
Doctor: 'Yes — how about bacon and onions?!'

'Doctor! Doctor! I feel like a television!'
'Do try and switch off!'

Where do pixies call in for medical treatment?
To the elf centre, when they're going gnome!

'Doctor! Doctor! I'm a little hoarse.'
'Neigh, lad, you're perfectly alright!'

Bill: 'Doctor, I'm coming down with the flue today.'
Doctor: 'Bah! You'd better hurry up and finish installing my central heating boiler!'
Bill: 'That's what I just said — I'm bringing the flue with me!'

Liz: 'Doctor, I get so nervous and frightened during driving tests!'
Doctor: 'Never mind. You'll pass eventually.'
Liz: 'But I'm the examiner!'

What d'you call a man who's swallowed a sack of potatoes?
    Spud!

'Doctor! Doctor! You don't seem to have much patience . . .'
    'That's because I have too many patients!'

'I won't say my doctor's incompetent — but he makes his patients sign an indemnity clause!'

'Doctor! Doctor! I feel like a bottle of beer . . .'
    'So do I! Let's go to the pub!'

Dave: I've been thinking of taking up playing the trumpet to calm my nerves. D'you think it's a good idea?'
Doctor: 'Why not? You don't live next-door to me!'

Madge: 'My Joe hadn't seen the doctor in thirty years till yesterday.'
Gladys: 'He must be very healthy . . .'
Madge: 'No, it was his post-mortem!'

What's big and scaly, aggressive, breathes fire and fears no man?
    A doctor's receptionist!

What d'you get if you swallow a feather duster?
    A tickle in the throat!

'Doctor! Doctor! I feel like a pair of false teeth . . .'
    'Never mind — keep smiling!'

Bill: 'I'm worn out after my wife made me move house at the weekend . . .'
Doctor: 'It shouldn't have been that much of a strain.'
Bill: 'But it was! She made me move it two metres to the left!'

'Doctor! Doctor! I feel like a watch.'
   'Don't get wound up about it!'

'Mr Hardacre, my prescription for you is simply a good holiday . . .'
   'Fine, doctor — now you can simply prescribe £500 to pay for it!'

'Doctor! Doctor! I can't stop eating raw onions day and night . . .'
   'Now, now! That's nothing to cry about!'

Joyce: 'I'm worried about my husband. He stands on his flower bed attending to his plants all day long.'
Doctor: 'Don't worry. Lots of people like gardening.'
Joyce: 'But we've only got a window box — on the 27th floor!'

Dick: 'I'm suffering from car-sickness.'
Doctor: 'Do you travel a lot by car?'
Dick: 'No, that's the whole point. My car won't go — and I'm sick of it!'

'Doctor! Doctor! I'm worried about my new boyfriend. He's in the marines — and someone's told me they're half soldiers and half sailors!'

Tom: 'Will you sign my passport photo, doctor?'
Doctor: 'Certainly not. I refuse to handle offensive material!'

What d'you call a man who's died from drinking too much whisky?
   Dead drunk!

'Doctor! Doctor! I keep thinking I'm a kettle . . .'
   'Don't get steamed up about it!'

What d'you call a woman who's swallowed a dictionary?
   Chatty!

Vic: 'Doctor, my fear of heights is stopping me from getting to the top of my profession . . .'
Doctor: 'And what is that?'
Vic: 'I'm a window cleaner!'

Mavis: 'My son is fourteen years old and he still can't tell the time.'
Doctor: 'Oh, I wonder why that is?'
Mavis: 'Our clock hasn't worked for the past fifteen years!'

'Doctor! Doctor! I feel like a yo-yo . . .'
  'Well, life has its ups and downs!'

Mary: 'Doctor, have you time to make a home visit today?'
Doctor: 'Of course, if it's really necessary.'
Mary: 'It is — I need help putting up my new kitchen shelves!'

Sue: 'Doctor, is it true that eating fish makes you brainy?'
Doctor: 'There's certainly some truth in that . . .'
Sue: 'So *that's* why our cat's just won Mastermind!'

'Doctor! Doctor! I have a plant growing out of my head!'
'Oh, dear! You must have gone to seed!'

What d'you call a clumsy doctor who drops the transfusion bottles?
A blood clot!

Millie: 'Doctor, I'm so unhappy. My husband is nothing but a wolf in sheep's clothing.'
Doctor: 'How extraordinary! Wouldn't you have preferred to marry a man?!'

Doctor: 'You're not very fit, Mr Windbag. I'm surprised at your condition, especially as you say you spend a lot of time playing sport.'

Windbag: 'Oh, I do, doctor. I play snooker on Mondays and Wednesdays, chess on Tuesdays and Thursdays, and darts at the weekend!'

Mrs Drudge: 'Will you ask the doctor to make a home visit this morning.'

Receptionist: 'He'll be round as soon as he can.'

Mrs Drudge: 'It'll have to be before eleven. I've got the shopping to do!'

June: 'I can't get any rest with my husband's snoring.'

Doctor: 'Get him to sleep in a different position.'

June: 'Like what?'

Doctor: 'In the garage!'

'Doctor! Doctor! I took the plunge and married Ivy last week — but I can't stand the sight of her.'

'Don't worry, she'll grow on you!'

Doctor: 'Tongue out, please . . . goodness, what a funny colour! I must ring the hospital at once!'
Sue: 'It's okay, doctor. I've just been eating a licorice stick!'

'Doctor! Doctor! The baby goat's chewed up my tablets . . .'
  'You're kidding!'

Edna: 'I have a bad back. Can you give me some liniment?'
Nurse: 'Certainly. Walk this way, please.'
Edna: 'If I could walk that way, I wouldn't need the liniment.'

Psychiatrist: 'I'm afraid you have a split personality.'
Mr Blenkinsop: 'That makes two of us!'

What's the difference between a docker and a doctor?
  One works on ships, the other on wrecks!

'Doctor! Doctor! If I bathe in milk every day, will I have pleasing skin?'
  'Your milkman will find it pleasing!'

'Doctor! Doctor! Will you give me something for my throat?'

'No, sorry — I don't want another throat, thank you!'

'A definite case of spring fever!'

'My doctor told me to eat plenty of fibre, but I find bits of cloth and balls of wool hard to swallow!'

'Doctor! Doctor! I've been a widow for twenty years now. Where should I look for a new husband?'
'The Isle of Man!'

'Doctor! Doctor! I keep dreaming I'm a shopkeeper . . .'
'Serves you right!'

Doctor: 'Your baldness is an hereditary condition, Mr Green.'
Mr Green: 'But, doctor, I have no heirs!'

A man waiting in the surgery is amazed to see a tiny little man in a white coat climb out of a drawer and walk across the desk to him.
'Who the heck are you?!' asks the patient.
'Look here,' growls the tiny man angrily. 'Do you want a micro-surgeon or not?!'

Doctor: 'That's a nasty cough you have, Elsie. I'll give you a bottle for it . . .'
Elsie: 'Huh! You might *fill* it for me, you old miser!'

'Doctor! Doctor! Those pills you gave me tasted delicious!'
  'Ah, so that's where my jelly-beans went!'

Ida: 'Take a look at my face, doctor. It's killing me.'
Doctor: 'It's not doing me much good either!'

Mr Twitty: 'Doctor, don't you agree that children should show respect for their teacher?'
Doctor: 'Of course.'
Mr Twitty: 'Then why are the kids so rude to me?'
Doctor: 'YOU — a teacher?! Ha, ha! Ho, ho! You can't be serious!'

'Doctor! Doctor! Everything is getting on my nerves . . .'
  'Well, don't leave them lying around!'

Doctor: 'Well, I've given you a thorough examination, Bill . . .'
Bill: 'What's the next step?'
Doctor: 'That's *your* funeral!'

Tom: 'Doctor! Horses make me itch and sneeze . . .'
Doctor: 'Well, stay away from them.'
Tom: 'I can't — I'm a jockey!'

Madge: 'I'm upset, doctor. That lady from next-door has been stealing from my dustbin again — and she chases me away when I try to stop her.'
Doctor: 'How shocking! What kind of a woman is she?'
Madge: 'Lady's not a woman — she's an Alsatian!'

'Doctor! Doctor! Would plastic surgery improve my looks?'
  'Who nose?!'

Softie: 'Can you prescribe me some seasickness pills for the afternoon?'
Doctor: 'Oh, are you going on holiday today?'
Softie: 'No, I'm taking a rowing boat out on the park lake!'

'Doctor! Doctor! I've got a singing noise in my ear.'
  'Lucky you! I have to turn the radio on first!'

David: 'Are girls as clever as boys, doctor?'
Doctor: 'They certainly are!'
David: 'Good, my sister can do my maths homework then!'

Maestro: 'While I was leading the orchestra, I slipped and fell off the stage and smashed into the floodlights . . .'
Doctor: 'Good job you're a bad conductor — or you could have been electrocuted!'

Lager lout: 'Doc, I can't stop mugging people, burgling houses and smashing bus shelters. What do you recommend for me?'
Doctor: 'Youth-anasia!'

Beattie: 'Sorry I brought you out to my husband, doctor. It was a false alarm.'
Doctor: 'But you said he was foaming at the mouth . . .'
Beattie: 'No, he'd just fallen asleep eating a cream cake!'

'Doctor! Doctor! I think I'm a pair of shoes . . .'
 'Stroll on!'

'You're barmy, Mr Watts . . .'
  'No, I'm not, doctor — look, I have a certificate to prove it!'

Rob: 'Aargh! Help me, doctor!'
Doctor: 'Do keep still — I'll soon find out what's wrong with you!'
Rob: 'I *know* what's wrong — my brother put itching powder in the talc shaker!'

'Doctor! Doctor! I have an awful barking cough. Would a holiday do me good?'
  'Maybe. Try the Isle of Dogs!'

What's worse than a pain in the leg?
  A pain in both legs!

'Doctor! Doctor! Why do I get a terrible headache whenever I go into the open air?'
  'Your hat's too tight!'

PC Catchum: 'Don't you think I look remarkably young for my age, doctor?'
Doctor: 'Sorry, I refuse to answer — on the grounds that I may incriminate myself!'

'Doctor! Doctor! I feel like a light bulb!'
  'Look on the bright side!'

Sue: 'If I rub myself all over with cod liver oil, will it make my skin look better?'
Doctor: 'I don't know about that, but it could be very dangerous — you might get licked to death by all the neighbourhood cats!'

'I was so worried about getting "Spanish tummy" on holiday, I came back with malnutrition!'

'Doctor! Doctor! I feel like a football . . .'
  'Well, don't let people kick you around!'

Tim: 'Doctor, I've just fallen off a bus!'
Doctor: 'How distressing for you . . .'
Tim: 'I'll say it is — I didn't get my change from the conductor!'

Mary: 'Doctor! Doctor! The hairdresser's ruined my hair — it's gone all different colours! What can I do?'
Doctor: 'Turn it to your advantage — get a job as a clown!'

Which bank do you put something in, and other people take it out?
   A blood bank!

'Doctor! Doctor! I think I'm a sapling . . .'
   'You'll grow out of it!'

Alf: 'When I criticised my wife's cooking, she hit me with a pancake.'
Doctor: 'That shouldn't have hurt you.'
Alf: 'But it was still in the frying pan!'

'Doctor! Doctor! I think I'm a clothes line!'
   'You need taking down a peg or two!'

Gladys: 'Grandad's going a bit peculiar. He puts horse manure on his rhubarb . . .'
Doctor: 'Well?'
Gladys: 'The rest of us put custard on ours!'

'Our doctor says new-born babies are like the weather — wet and windy.'

Joe: 'Do you believe we're descended from apes, doctor?'
Doctor: 'I do now that I've examined *you*!'

Billy: 'I've just swallowed a pound coin, doctor.'
Doctor: 'It should pass through your system, Billy.'
Billy: 'Can you lend me another one, and I'll give you mine when I get it back?'

'Doctor! Doctor! My wife's colour blindness is causing problems. For last night's supper we had eggs with chips made from apples!'

'Doctor! Doctor! I feel like a worn-out dish-cloth . . .'
'Really? Well chew it well; they're awfully difficult to digest!'

'Doctor! Doctor! I think I'm a book!'
'Try and turn over a new leaf!'

Doctor: 'Can you describe this ringing in your ears, Miss White?'
Miss White: 'Yes, doctor. It sounds like seaside donkeys jangling along the beach . . .'
Doctor: 'Then what on earth are you complaining about? What could be more pleasant than imagining you're at the seaside all year round?!'

Why is a boring newspaper like someone with chilblains?
They both have poor circulation!

Ted: 'My wife's driving is killing me, doctor.'
Doctor: 'Well, don't get in the car with her.'
Ted: 'I don't have to. She nearly ran me over yesterday, reversing out of the garage!'

Sue: 'What's the secret of good health?'
Doctor: 'I dunno, but I hope no one discovers it — or I'll be out of a job!'

'Doctor! Doctor! I think I'm a shoe . . .'
  'It might help if you didn't look so down-at-heel!'

Joe: 'I've got terrible earache. I'd better move house.'
Doctor: 'Why?'
Joe: 'It's next-door's stereo that's doing it!'

'Doctor! Doctor! My brother and I have this urge to hang upside-down in dark caves. What's wrong with us?'
  'I'd say you were bats!'

'Doctor! — Er — Doctor! — I — um — I think I'm — er, well – a flag!'
'Stop wavering, will you?!'

Billy: 'Doctor, I've taken too much castor oil and . . .'
Doctor: 'Come back, Billy! Don't run off like that!'

'Doctor! Doctor! I'm desperate! I'm going bald!'
'Now, now, keep your hair on!'

Luigi: 'Since I retired, I do nothing all day but sit and eat spaghetti . . .'
Doctor: 'You're obviously pasta your besta!'

Ethel: 'I get seriously out of breath when I go up the stairs.'
Doctor: 'That sounds bad. How many stairs do you climb?'
Ethel: 'Fifteen flights — the lift's out of order!'

'Doctor! Doctor! My ambition to become a famous writer is making me ill!'
'Cheer up, I'm sure you'll make it in the end, Mr Shakespeare!'

'Doctor! Doctor! You have a thriving career, a beautiful wife, a lovely home and pots of money. How do you do it?'
  'With great style!'

'Doctor! Doctor! I've been bitten by a bed bug!'
  'Snap — I've been bitten by the travel bug. I'll see to you on my return from the Seychelles!'

'Doctor keeps it to cure patients with hiccups!'

Fred: 'Bah! My brother's got me the sack. I told him to ring the boss to say I was feeling bilious.'
Doctor: 'Yes?'
Fred: 'He said I was playing billiards!'

'Doctor! Doctor! I feel like a piece of fish!'
'Sounds like you've had your chips!'

Doctor: 'Take my advice and avoid eating raw eggs.'
Jeannie: 'But my cake icing won't taste the same made with hard-boiled eggs!'

Farmer Giles: 'I've used all your ointments, doctor, but my legs are still chapped at the top.'
Doctor: 'In that case I think you'd better consider cutting a couple of inches off the top of your wellies!'

Jim: 'Help me! I've gone and eaten a paperweight instead of one of my wife's rock cakes!'
Doctor: 'I find that difficult to believe . . .'
Jim: 'You've not tasted her rock cakes!'

'Doctor! Doctor! I think I'm a bar of soap!'
'Don't get into a lather about it!'

'I can't help thinking Dr Lawton is in the wrong kind of theatre!'

'Doctor! Doctor! After I've been gardening I get terrible aches in my arms and legs. What are they?'
'Growing pains!'

Where can you see more doctors than in a hospital?
   On a golf course!

'Doctor! Doctor! I keep dreaming I'm a comedian.'
   'You're joking!'

Doctor: 'Of course you're fit for work, Mr Idleloff. Hard work never killed anyone.'
Idleloff: 'It killed my Uncle Ivan.'
Doctor: 'Nonsense! Where did he work?'
Idleloff: 'Down a Siberian salt mine!'

Patient: 'Did you always want to be a brain surgeon?'
Doctor: 'No. I tried to be a plumber but I couldn't pass the tests!'

'Doctor! Doctor! My wife's a cleaning fanatic. What can I do?'
   'Send her round to see me. My cleaner's useless!'

'Mr Sozzle — when I told you a couple of whiskies a week wouldn't do you any harm, I didn't mean a couple of *bottles*!'

What do you get if you eat your horse's dinner?
   Hay fever!

'Doctor! Doctor! I feel like I'm a tube of toothpaste!'
   'Don't let anyone give you the brush-off!'

'Doctor! Doctor! I'm so depressed. If I were rich, would I be happy?'
   'Perhaps not, but you could be miserable in comfort!'

Pat: 'You must help my grandad. He can't stop growing potatoes and cauliflowers.'
Doctor: 'Nothing wrong with that . . .'
Pat: 'Out of his ears?!!'

'Doctor! Doctor! My legs tremble like jelly and custard. Is it a serious condition?'
   'No, just a mere trifle!'

When is a baby bad tempered?
   When it's been given gripe water!

'I'm a bit worried about this new anaesthetist!'

'Doctor! Doctor! I think I'm a match!'
  'Cor, strike a light!'

Why is a sore eye like a pig?
  They both have sties!

'Doctor! Doctor! I feel like a spinning-wheel. I hope you can help me.'
  'Right, let's get weaving!'

Sharon: 'My boyfriend says my skin's like a peach . . .'
Doctor: 'Mmm, all yellow and hairy!'
Sharon: 'And my teeth are like the stars . . .'
Doctor: 'Yes, they come out at night!'

'Doctor! Doctor! I was pouring in sweat last night.'
  'Try turning off the electric blanket!'

'Doctor! Doctor! Do you know the secret of eternal youth?'
  'No, and by the look of you, neither do *you*!'

Frank: 'Doctor, how do you become rich and handsome?'
Doctor: 'Oh, I guess I was just born that way!'

'Doctor! Doctor! Is there any way I can keep my wrinkles at bay?'
  'I suppose you could live on a boat in the sea at Morecambe!'

'Doctor! Doctor! I think I'm a doormat.'
  'You must stop letting people walk all over you!'

Betty: 'Where's Doctor Jones?'
Doctor: 'I'm afraid he's away for a few days; I'm his locum.'
Betty: 'Oh, you must be Doc Holiday then!'

Gladys: 'I fell and bruised my knee — it's turning all different shades of blue, green, yellow and purple.'
Doctor: 'Let me see . . . ah, yes, now that's exactly the colour scheme I want for my drawing-room!'

Jack: 'My wife's punched me and given me a fat lip, doctor.'
Doctor: 'Don't worry, it's quite in keeping with the rest of you!'

Doctor: 'What can I do for you, Miss Smith?'
Carol: 'It's not Miss Smith any more, doctor — last week I married a Swede I met on holiday . . .'
Doctor: 'Oh, good, at least you'll never go hungry!'

'Doctor! Doctor! I keep having funny turns.'
  'Really? I'll have to hire you for my son's birthday party!'

Emily: 'Am *I* glad you've called, doctor. I'm going mad with this terrible noise in my ear!'
Doctor: 'Silly! It's your smoke-alarm — the battery needs changing!'

'Doctor! Doctor! I keep wetting myself. What shall I do?'
 'Well, whatever you do, don't remove your bicycle clips in here!'

Agatha: 'I'd like to invite you to accompany me on my trip to America . . .'
Doctor: 'That's very nice. Why me?'
Agatha: 'I've heard it can be very expensive to see a doctor once you get there!'

Stan: 'My tummy's getting awful big, doctor.'
Doctor: 'I agree. You should diet.'
Stan: 'Really? What colour?'

Doctor: 'I'd like to inform you that you're in tip-top condition . . .'
Tom: 'How wonderful!'
Doctor: 'I'd *like* to inform you of that — but I can't! You'll be dead tomorrow!'

Cannibal: 'Did you know, doctor — I've brought up sixteen children?'
Witch-doctor: 'Then try eating them more slowly!'

Walter: 'I'm getting married next week, doctor. Any advice?'
Doctor: 'Yes — don't!'

'Doctor! Doctor! I think I'm a postage stamp.'
   'Oh, dear! That's a sticky problem!'

Doctor: 'I'm sorry to hear your husband died in his bubble-car, Mrs Brown. What happened?'
Mrs Brown: 'It burst at 60 mph!'

Doctor: 'Eat plenty of apples, Mr Skinflint.'
Skinflint: 'Not likely! I read that apples are composed mainly of water!'
Doctor: 'Er — yes, I think they are . . .'
Skinflint: 'Well, I'm not paying 60p a pound for water when I can get it free from the tap!'

'Doctor! Doctor! I've got a running sore . . .'
  'Try and catch up with it and then slap a plaster on!'

Psychiatrist: 'You read too much into things people say to you. Now relax and enjoy a cup of tea with . . .'
Mr Robinson: 'And what exactly do you mean by that?!!'

What did Doctor Watson say when Sherlock found it hard to swallow?
  'Alimentary, my dear fellow!'

Victoria: 'When I sit on my pony, my toes curl up, doctor.'
Doctor: 'Try a size larger in tights!'

Doctor: 'Hello, Mrs Jones. Is your hubby any fitter since I advised him to take up swimming?'
Mrs Jones: 'Not really — he drowned last week!'

'I don't understand why I can't sleep at night, doctor. After all, I'm up by 11am each morning and I've cut my afternoon nap down to three hours!'

'A man died instantly today from an art attack — when a bronze statue fell on him!'

Sam: 'So, carrots are full of vitamins, eh?'
Doctor: 'That's right — "A".'
Sam: 'Eh?'
Doctor: 'Aye, "A"!'
Sam: 'Oh!'

'Doctor! Doctor! I've made a self-diagnosis — I think I'm an encyclopedia!'
   'Now, don't be such a know-all!'

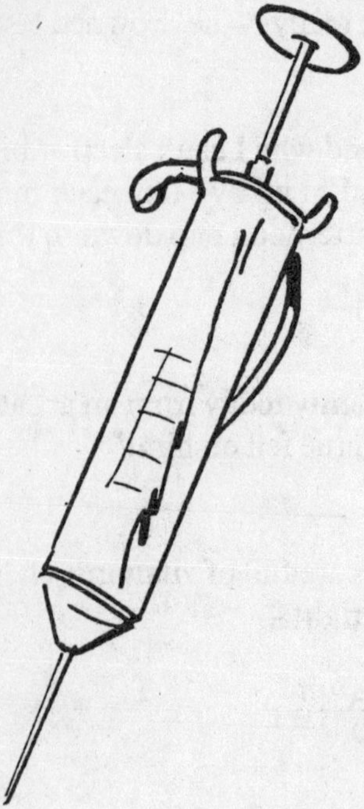